About the Author

LAURA HAWRYLUCK received her MD from the University of Western Ontario where she served her Internal Medicine residency. She completed a Fellowship in Critical Care at the University of Manitoba and MSc. in Bioethics from the University of Toronto, Canada. Associate Professor of Critical Care Medicine at the University of Toronto, she was awarded the Queen's Golden Jubilee Medal for contributions to Canada in improving end of life care, the Medico-Legal Society of Toronto award for contributions to health law, and the University of Toronto Interdepartmental Critical Care Medicine Humanitarian Award for her contributions to international humanitarian work.

An ICU Doctor's Reflections

Dr. Laura A. Hawryluck

An ICU Doctor's Reflections

Olympia Publishers
London

www.olympiapublishers.com
OLYMPIA PAPERBACK EDITION

Copyright © Dr. Laura A. Hawryluck 2020

The right of Dr. Laura A. Hawryluck to be identified as author of this work has been asserted in accordance with sections 77 and 78 of the Copyright, Designs and Patents Act 1988.

All Rights Reserved

No reproduction, copy or transmission of this publication may be made without written permission.
No paragraph of this publication may be reproduced, copied or transmitted save with the written permission of the publisher, or in accordance with the provisions of the Copyright Act 1956 (as amended).

Any person who commits any unauthorised act in relation to this publication may be liable to criminal prosecution and civil claims for damage.

A CIP catalogue record for this title is available from the British Library.

ISBN: 978-1-78830-660-7

First Published in 2020

Olympia Publishers
Tallis House
2 Tallis Street
London
EC4Y 0AB

Printed in Great Britain

Dedication

For Edith, Stan and Chris
For not losing patience,
When I began to rhyme
For a certain time.

For Pam
To voice the inexpressible truths
Who told me I could write,
And who just may have been right.

For my ICU family working the clinical frontlines across the globe
For always bringing humanity to the fights we wage
Being who you are, every single day,
Means much more than my words could ever say.

For my patients and their families
Thank you for your inspiration.
You always have all my respect and admiration.

Introduction

I wrote this collection of poems to capture some of the very personal moments of lives lived within the intensive care unit (ICU). I tried to provide pictures of critical illness and its impact on the lives of patients and their families. I hope I have captured the fears, worry and heartbreaks as well as the courage, love and joy, we, patients, families and healthcare providers live through every day. I wrote this to explore the lessons I have learned as a doctor and as a tribute to all those I have cared for.

Having been a patient myself—though not in the ICU—and having lost my own friends and family members in the ICU, I have written from a variety of different perspectives, in a variety of voices. Through these voices I hope readers will reflect on who they are and what matters to them in life. For the answers to these questions are the very things that should be considered when making treatment/healthcare decisions of any kind—and in particular when making any high-stake treatment choices.

Before you reach a time in your life when you need to make healthcare decisions of your own, I hope these reflections will help you have your own meaningful conversations with those you love.

In My Shoes

Would you choose to walk a mile in my shoes?
Through broken bodies and minds
From illnesses of every kind.

Would you care,
Or just stop and stare
At other's misfortunes?

Would you have the strength to be patient and kind,
Or would your behaviour be of quite another kind?

It takes courage to see the tears and fears.
It takes courage to see the anguish and pain
And the love that always remains.

It takes courage to admit to losing the fight
After being awake all night.

It takes resilience to continue and hope for better days.
To believe you will once again see the sun's rays.

It takes courage to share,
Courage to care.
Would you dare?

Lines

The line is so very thin;
The chances are so very slim.

Treatments are flirting
Between helping and hurting.
Where is the line between living and dying?
Where is the line between trying and sighing?

What is a doctor to do?
What does it mean to treat you?

Don't you wish you were able
To sit at a philosopher's table?

But hard decisions need to be made:
Can your life be saved?

Illness

Illness comes to us all:
Homeless, poor or professional.
Being rich grants no protection
From being caught in its selection.

Illness can decimate health
Regardless of wealth,
I know it's hard for you to face
But power does not grant you grace.
Demands for speedy solutions
By throwing your weight around,
Is no way to achieve resolutions.
Illness brings everyone to the ground.

Illness does not care if you are smart.
Illness will still tear you apart.
Illness does not care if you are strong.
Illness will make you understand this is wrong.
For you will be tested
And, at least for a while, you will be bested.

You no longer have the con,
You are just a pawn
Now you are living your greatest fears.
It's only normal you are brought to tears.

I know you will dislike this
But illness is like this.
Reflect—for this is true,
I have no reason to lie to you.

Illness helps us all understand
Why we need each other's helping hand.
Now, maybe you can learn to understand
Your fellow Man.

Being a Doctor

I listen to your story,
I do a physical exam,
I need to understand
So that I can do what I can.

Before your health can be restored,
Your signs and symptoms must be explored.
I test, I treat, I repeat;
For re-evaluation
Is the key to your salvation.

I must be complete.
There are no shortcuts, no ways to cheat.
I must always be pensive
In order to be comprehensive.

Now that we have a diagnosis,
Now that we understand the prognosis,
I know what to do
To get you through.

Now you are healed and on your way,
You are leaving the hospital today
And I listen to your story, your future dreams.
Sometimes life is really as good as it seems.

What Would You Choose?

What would you choose
If death suddenly roamed around your edges,
Just when you thought you had escaped its ledges?

Would you fly to the sky
And live each day knowing life will never be stable,
Or risk death on an operating table?
While the diciest of surgery may stave off your mortality
Is such a choice real or a challenge to morality?

What would you choose if this was your fate?
The joys and strife of an extraordinary life
Or death on a predetermined certain date?

Would you have the courage to use your wings?
Or spend your life on a swing,
Between hope and despair,
Will I find you there?

Hope

Hope burns bright in the emergency lights.
Hope for caring and compassion,
Hope for curing as a passion.

Hope to be restored to health,
Hope for the greatest of wealth.

Hope to make it all go away.
The hope for healing
Can get many kneeling and dealing,
And even as hope slips away,
Many still always hope for a new day.

Hope always burns bright
In the darkness of the night.

Trust

Do you trust me to help you heal?
How would this thought make you feel?

Trust is earned
But bridges are easily burned.

Preconceived notions can deceive;
What would it take for you to believe?

Honesty, clarity and caring
Are what we need to be sharing.

For trust arises
If we can avoid too many surprises.

To Offer or not to Offer

To offer or not to offer.
What does it mean?
The answer is not as easy as it would seem.

How can I help more than I hurt?
What treatment options exist
To get you through this illness?
What does research reveal?
How can I help you heal?

How can I help more than I hurt?
Where is the line that I must define?
In the context of your state of health,
Will these treatments save your self?
Or will they achieve something else?

To offer or not to offer? I ask.
It is not a simple task.
The issues are complex
And the answers depend on the context.

Your Mom

I can see you are bitter
And I can see your eyes glitter,
As I come to greet you,
As I come to meet you.

Your mother is in the hospital bed.
Her long list of problems show the road she has traveled,
Before it all came unraveled.
As you describe her issues,
I grab you a box of tissues.
I can see your dread
At what lies ahead.

You are right to fight
For she is not just a broken body in a bed.
With snowy locks upon her head,
She is your mother,
You have no other.

I want to be clear.
I am here to help the mom you hold dear.
She deserves all our respect,
She is worthy of much more than she often gets.

Here is what I can do to help.
Here is what I cannot do
For it would hurt her,
And it would hurt you too.

So instead of bringing her to the ICU,
Bringing the ICU to her is what we will do.
For it's my intention
To give your mom the utmost care and attention.

I hope we can work together
To try to get your mom better.
We take pride in what we do
And we hope you will too.

High Standards

I have high standards you say.
Well… would you want it any other way?

You treat everyone as V.I.P.
Well… why shouldn't that be?
Shouldn't that be right
When they come in sick in the night?

Every one of us has a story.
Every care is worthy of glory.
No one should be treated like they don't matter at all.
Well… wouldn't you want me to give it my all?

My Doctor

I look for you in deepest night,
I look for you in dawn's first light,
I look for you in your machines' red glare,
I look for you in your cold, hard stare.

I look for you in the depths of your heart,
I look for you as you tear apart,
I look for you in the depths of your despair.
If I look long enough will I find you there?

I look for you in your loss of vanity.
I look for you in the rebirth of your humanity.
I hope to see you there,
I hope to see you care.

Healthcare in the Media

See the dark clouds roaming,
In the light of the gloaming.

See the darkness fall,
In the light that fails us all.

See the loss of humanity
And the dawn of profanity.

See the loss of appreciation
For whom we are and what we know.
The devaluation of what we bring
To lives we are meant to be helping.

Is it justified?
Well… what are *you* doing to keep the faith in medicine alive?

See the loss of light.
Do something to keep it burning bright.

Decisions

Do you want CPR and life support?
How do I know? I retort.
What does this all involve?
I feel your questions are a mystery to be solved.

If your heart stops, do you want everything done?
I know I must look kind of stunned.
Of course, I would want you to try;
I would like to stay alive.

Instead of asking me about a medical life,
We could avoid all this strife.
We could start by simply speaking
And you could ask me what I am seeking.
How did we arrive
At all this pressure to decide?

Ask me what I do,
What values and beliefs I hold true.
Ask me about my stories
And what joys life brings.
Ask me what makes my heart sing.

Ask me about my dreams
And what tears me apart at the seams.
Ask me about my fears
And what brings me to tears.
Ask me what I can't live without

Then ask me if I have any doubt.
For if all this you discover
We can really talk with each other,
You will have the keys to see what it means to be me
And what I would like my life to be.

If we understand each other,
You will help me see what our journey together will hold;
How the rest of my life will unfold.

Consent

I need to know if you are able
To understand what I am putting on the table.
We need to decide quick,
For you are so very sick.

Life support and resuscitation are not easy to explain,
So, let me be very plain,
Of breathing and feeding tubes, machines and monitors I speak.
Of medicines such as adrenaline
That need monitoring and titration.
Of pain control and sedation,
Of the frustrations and loss of communication.
Of risks and side effects,
Of irritations and complications
And all the alarms that go beep.
That don't allow you to really sleep.

While I do not know how long
Before all this would once again be gone,
I do need to explain,
And again, be very plain,
If we are not resuscitating
We will be palliating.

I need you to understand you have a choice,
And I need to hear your voice,
For I do not want to put you through
Things you do not want to do
Or things that don't mean much to you.

I know this is a lot to grasp,
Especially when for every breath you gasp,
Do you understand what I am treating?
What are the goals you are seeking?

What is your quality of life?
Quick, there is no time to think twice.

A life you hate

Time goes by so swiftly.
Life nears its end so quickly.
So, tell me how you want to live,
Not what treatments you want me to give.
Living a life you hate
Is a most terrible fate.

It's not a question of living or dying.
A point has been reached,
A line has been breached
And life as you know it can't be restored.
And life as you know it is changed for evermore.

When you can no longer speak,
Others will talk about the life you seek.
They won't want to stop treating
When we say you are dying;
They will say we are lying.
So, tell me how you want to live,
Not what treatments you want me to give.
Living a life you would hate
Is a most terrible fate.

The line between living and dying is so very thin
And what it means for you to live
Should direct any treatment we give.
Day and night, night and day.
Sometimes it's life we should fear,
When death is so very near.
Forced to live a life you hate
Is the most terrible fate.

Call

Did you see the warning signs?
The change in his vital signs?
His heart raced, his blood pressure fall;
Why did you not call?

When you see such deterioration-
Call
Without hesitation.
Failure of recognition shouldn't happen at all-
Call.

Before I leave to bring him to the ICU,
I have these words to say to you.
There is no need for trepidation at all-
Call.
I will share your worry,
I will be there in a hurry.

I need to trust you
In order to rescue.
On it depends his fate,
So please do not hesitate;
Escalate.
Don't hesitate at all-
Call.

Always thinking

Through endless calls and crowded halls;
Thinking, thinking, thinking.

Through sleepless nights and hallway lights;
Thinking, thinking, thinking.

Through constant noise, as I struggle to keep my poise;
Thinking, thinking, thinking.

Can I fix your broken self?
Can I restore you to health?
Thinking, thinking, thinking.

What more can I do,
What else do I need to pursue
To cure you?

Suicide

Your life is such a success.
It's all people see.
No one could guess
Inside, you feel such a mess.
So worthless;
How could it be,
That no one can see?

You seem happy and smile,
Though all the while
You are planning to die
By suicide.

Lost and alone, you waited 'til no one was home.
By sheer luck you were found,
Before you completely ran aground.

From far and wide, people who hold you dear
Now appear.
And as they draw near,
One question becomes a refrain,
One question spreads like a runaway train.

Why?

Why did you want to cease to be?
Why did they not see?
Why did you not feel the love you were shown?

Why was no one else home?
Why did you feel so much despair?
Why were they not there?
Why did you think they did not care?
Why did they not see?
That you were going to try to die
By suicide.

So many questions, no answers found.
Guilt and blame surround.
So much hurt and pain all around.
No answers can be found.

Though you are here,
Heavily sedated
In your ICU bed,
No one, including me,
Can answer what was going through your head.

But… you did not succeed.
Though so many people now bleed
A river of despair,
Now shared.
And… though it's now buried deep,
Hope, such a little seed
Now shared,
Can still burn bright
In the darkness of your night.

The Code

I must hide my inner turmoil,
Though my mind just wants to recoil.

What is happening to you?
How can this be true?

I need to compartmentalise,
To keep you alive
I need to analyse.
On this your survival depends.
On this, my focus expends.

The scene is hectic
And people frenetic.

I must stay calm;
I hold your life in my palm.

Getting through the night

Despite all the care and attention,
Despite the best of intentions,
I did not know if we could make it through the night.
I could not let you out of my sight.

Now that we have, it's time for me to leave
And for another team to help you breathe.
I will never forget how we forged a team, you and I,
And made it to the morning sky.

I do not know how your day will go.
I hope you get better though.
I hope I will see you again,
That you will be clearly on the mend,
That you will be whole once again.

The Substitute

You did not want to go to the Emergency Department;
I couldn't get you to leave the apartment.
One look…
It was all it took.
You were barely alive;
They didn't know if you would survive.

There was nothing I could say
Before they whisked you away.
There was no time for talking,
It was all so shocking.
While I was shaking
They were resuscitating.

Swirling, whirling, I try to register
Fractured moments that defy capture
What if I got you in sooner, what if?
Would you still be going through all this?
So surreal, I walk through your door
One look,
Was all it took
And I stare at the floor
Two haunting words… what if?

Now the doctors come by every day
And I don't know what to say.
What do I tell them to do?
How do I get through to you?

You and I spoke so much before

But never on this score.
Whenever I tried to talk about this
You closed every door,
Even if you did it with a kiss.
So now I wait for a sign
Of some grand design.
I hope I'll know it
When I see it.

Would you want all this?
Can I put you through it?
Or should I stop all this sustaining
And let you live any time remaining?

I feel an anguish
I just can't vanquish
And a fear I cannot hide,
As I sit by your bedside.

Please tell me what to do.
How do I get through to you?
And… well… what if?

The ICU Team

It takes a village to get you through the storm into the light.
It takes a village to make everything alright.

What is this village of which I speak?
Who are these people you must meet?
While their faces will blur in any of your recollections,
They work with tight interconnections.

For you and each other
They are a team like no other.
Through long days and nights, they struggle to save your life.
There is little time for inner strife;
For better or worse, a family they form.
One that is far beyond the usual norm.

While at their best, they work as one,
Each has their say;
No one would want it any other way,
For you would not live another day.

I stand alone

While they all have their say,
Decisions must be made at the end of the day,
For critical illness not to have its way.

Being a team leader is no easy feat.
This should be no surprise;
Critical illness I am trained to treat
And it's not easy to concede defeat.
This too should come as no surprise
If you open your eyes,
Through all this I must rise.

At the end of the day
I stand alone
And my heart is not made of stone.

Some decisions are final;
They cannot be reversed.
And at times like this I feel I am cursed.

Where do I begin?
I crawl inside your skin,
I listen to your voice,
I make a choice.

Risk

How much certainty in your prognosis,
Can I give you with your diagnosis?

You ask for numbers, percentages and statistics.
I try to explain that medicine is not mathematics.
Numbers do not tell an individual story;
For this I am very sorry.

Numbers cannot describe what road you will travel by,
Whether you will live
Or whether you will die.

How much risk are you willing to take
When decisions are so high stake?

Sleep you ask?

When do I sleep?
When the machines no longer beep.

I sleep when I go home,
I sleep when I am alone.

So many people want my attention;
Far too many to mention.
Their calls are a never-ending drone.
I often feel I should be cloned.

For you and your family I am here.
For all those you hold dear,
Until you no longer need me,
Until I can be me.

I Am Intensivist

"Nurse, nurse please come here.
Please come and help me my dear."
I am not a nurse, I sigh.
I am your doctor; I was just at your bedside.

"Oh, it's nice to meet you
What do you do?"
I work in an ICU.
"Ah, you must be a nurse.
Tell me is it a blessing or a curse?"

I try not to be terse.
I do not know if it's a curse,
For I am not a nurse.

I know it's not your fault,
You just believe the default.
Why does the world persist
In being so sexist?

What is worse is when it's more condescending,
With deprecations covered in dissimulations
And even flirtations.

Do not diminish my training,
For it was very draining,
With your gender-based assumptions
And the implication that I lack gumption.

Do not diminish my accomplishments
With your false compliments.
Do not underestimate my skills;
I do far more than just prescribe pills.

While I may display more emotions than my male
counterparts,
Do not worry I will not fall apart.
I can think.
And, thanks, I will tell *you* if I need a drink.
And no, I do not need *to take a pill,*
I assure you I am very far from being ill;
For I am more than able to cope;
No one needs to throw me a rope.

Respect me for what I have done.
Respect me for who I have become.
See me as second to none.

The time for change has come.
The time for sexism and bullying is done.

Free to be

I know it seems forever
That we have been together.
I am here to report
That we are weaning your support.
Do not roll your eyes,
It's true—I am not telling lies.

I know it is frustrating,
This lack of communicating.
But soon the tube will be gone.
You will be hoarse,
Your voice will be coarse,
But soon it will get strong
And you will be talking the whole night long.

I know you are longing
To be eating and drinking
And your mouth is so dry;
You just want to cry.
But soon the tube will be gone.
You will be swallowing
Without choking
And you will be eating and drinking
As much as you want.

Do not roll your eyes.
I see the frustration in your sighs
To you, I swear this is true.
Breathing on machines is not as easy as it seems.
Separating from the ventilator is not much better;
I get it can be scary
When you start to wean.

We are here to cheer you on.
Work with us and it won't be long
Before your need for support is gone
And then you will be free
To do what you want
And free to just be.

The Survivor

When we met you were so sick.
The news I had to break
Cut your family to the quick
And made my heart ache.

Onto life support you crashed
In your hard landing.
Many hopes were dashed
And few were left standing.

Ever so slowly you improved,
Though many thought you couldn't beat it.
Few dared repeat it.
Soon their doubt was disproved
And hope firmly seeded.

Now life support is coming off.
The news I have to break
Eases all heartache.

You won't remember who we are.
You won't remember our celebration,
Nor our hearts' elation.

For you, life begins anew
And we are so happy this is true,
Though you are a very different you.

Recovery

Don't tell me what I can do,
Let me be the one to tell you.

Don't tell what I can achieve.
You will be surprised at what I have up my sleeve.

Don't treat me like I am made of glass.
I am more than strong enough to last.

Let me rediscover my self;
I know I am changed,
That my life must be re-arranged.
But it's up to me to find my limit
And I can tell you now I won't live within it,
At least not for long
Because I intend to get strong.

Remember what I have been through,
Though my own memories are few.
This, *this*, I know is true,
I have survived the ICU.

The Addict

A life of pain and sorrow.
A life of escape
Lived as though there was no tomorrow.
A terrible prediction;
A life of addiction.

A life of crime
Was never your design,
But your addiction had to be fed
To escape the demons in your head.

You felt so empty inside.
You used drugs to hide
But you could not avoid
The deepest void,
The hole in your heart.
When did it all start?

A life-threatening dose,
Left you comatose,
Lost in an alley
In the darkest of valleys.
You started seizing,
Then you stopped breathing.

While you survive,
Once again you start to lie
And try to hide inside your head.
Embarrassed, ashamed,
Once again full of pain,
Once again full of dread.

But the truth can't be sold.
You need to be bold,
Your whole story needs to be told.
There is no more need to hide
All the emptiness inside.

The causes of your addiction must be faced squarely.
We understand very well that this is beyond scary.
We see who you are,
We see all your scars,
We need to understand your personal wars.
No matter what you share and what has come before,
We see someone worth fighting for.

We know you have been marginalised.
We know you have been stigmatised.
We can see the good in you;
We know it's there and true.

We have seen how those who love you wept.
Don't make all sorts of promises that can't be kept.
Please, please just take that first step;
It's much larger than it seems,
To connect with the Addictions team.

We will share your pride
As you start to live with a different stride.
We will keep our fingers crossed
And hope you will no longer feel lost.
We believe you can find a way
To live a new way, day after day.

We know it won't be easy.
We will always be rooting for you,
Hoping you will never again need the ICU.

Celebrate life

Don't let illness define who you are.
Live your life guided by a different star.

For you are more than the sum of your medical problems,
Even if your doctors can't solve them.

No one knows why illnesses strike,
But don't let them shut off your light.

You can't forget your illnesses and sorrows,
But focus on a better tomorrow.

Life is too short and you can't replace it.
Seek to understand its stories
And celebrate its glories.
Celebrate life;
Do not waste it.

Never let illness define who you are.
Live your life guided by a different star.

The Return

Four months in the ICU,
Five more on the floor,
Six in Rehab
And now I am really glad
To be opening this ICU door.
To see you all again once more.

It's been a long hard road
To be able to walk,
To be able to talk.
There were days I thought I would never get through.
Finally, here I am; standing, this time, in front of you.

Fractured recollections,
Lost in self-reflections.
As you gather 'round
It becomes hard for me to even make a sound.

You ask me what I remember;
Not much I fear,
Though I wish memories of your faces were more clear.
Who are you?
Do you know me? Do I know you?

I feel I owe you everything.
I don't know from where your kindness springs,
But I wish you more happiness then any life can bring.
I don't know what to say;

I owe you a debt I can never repay.
But as I see your smiles shine bright
I realise that through my return I bring you light.
Your delight in my recovery
Is quite a new discovery.

You ask me how I have been doing;
I tell you I am still improving.
Though my journey is so slow
I want you to know
That I am going to be fine.
It's just going to take some more time.

I came back to say thanks.
Such a simple word among those ever heard,
Yet it's teaming with a whole wealth of meaning,
That I hope you completely understand
As you shake my hand.

Handshakes and hugs all around,
A few pieces of my life found.
Too soon it's time to say goodbye,
Too soon it's time for me to fly.
I feel there are many things I should say;
Once again, it's hard for me to make a sound.
Scattered memories abound
As you all have gathered 'round.
But… I may be back to visit once again
Some day;
Who can say?

Health and Wealth

Wealth is not health,
Though many wish it so.

Health is not wealth,
Though many say it's so.

Health is not wealth,
Wealth is not health.
Do not look for either here;
The price of both is far too dear.

Wealth and health can both be found
If life is turned upside down.
Look for who you are.
Where is your North Star?
Truth and wisdom can be found;
Turn your life around.

Slipping Away

Every day you grow frailer,
Every day just a little paler.

I try to build fences
To shore up your defences.
You smile at me through your pain,
But every time we gain,
I feel it's all in vain.

Please meet me half-way
And together we will find a way.

Every day you get stronger
Is a chance of another day longer.

Please don't slip away.
Let's work together and rage our way
Into a brand-new day.
What do you say?

So far away…

Why did I have to move so far away?
You know it was for work they say,
But Dad is sick and may be dying;
I am crying
And I need to be flying.

Using Skype doesn't make it feel right.
I feel lost and alone
Even with my smartphone.
And intermittent connection
Does not give me a sense of direction.

What I really want is to stand
And hold your hand.
Why does it take so long to get to you,
When you are in the ICU?

The Advocate

Why aren't things going according to plan?
Do I need to take a stand?
Raise my voice?
Do I have a choice?
I just don't understand
Why things aren't going according to plan.

It's been one complication after another.
I don't think you can take any more.
I seem to be the only one keeping score.
Who do I go to, what do I say?
I can just feel you slipping away.

I can't bear to see you,
I don't know how to help you.
Do I believe their diagnosis and prognosis?
Or is it a second opinion I should seek?
Should I speak?

I don't want to offend,
But I just can't pretend
That all is fine;
When I think I am losing my mind.

Best Intentions

I know you want to help.
Sharing stories of extraordinary revival,
Means nothing for his survival.
They just make me want to yelp.

I know you want to give me hope
But these stories don't help me cope.
I know your intentions are the best
But I really need you to give it a rest.

I can't rely on such stories;
Such tales of glories,
When doctors were so wrong.
It became a song.

I need to trust what I am being told.
His illness is making me so tired and old.
I don't know how to rest,
I don't know how to pass this test.

Please just stay with me for a while.
Let's just reminisce
About all the things I miss.
Please just stay with me for a while;
Please just help me smile.

The Fighter

He is a fighter, they say,
Despite the news we must impart.
They do not believe
Illness will tear him apart.

Around the clock we bear witness
To the ravages of his illness,
To his suffering and pain.
We know he will never be the same again.

Now we must report,
We need to increase his support
To try to save his life.
But oh, at what a price?

It is no longer a question of will but of ability,
Despite medical science's agility.
There is always a point where it can't overcome our body's fragility.

He is a fighter, they insist.
I have no doubt this is true,
But now there is nothing I can do.
I cannot cure or stabilise with escalation.
I am left with alleviation and palliation,
With a lot more sedation.

Medical science has reached its limits,
I know this is hard to hear,
I know this is hard to bear.
It's not that I don't care
And I am so very sorry to report,
That the time has come to withdraw life support.

I do not want to fight;
I just want to do what's right.
An instrument of harm, medicine should never be,
If it's to remain true to you and me.

Miracles

We believe in miracles,
We know they are true.
The internet is full of stories
That we will share with you.
We know you don't believe,
For reasons we just can't conceive.

We have been told over and over
That all hope is gone.
But we believe you are all wrong;
We must remain strong.

Our beliefs will see us through.
We know this is true.
We don't want to fight,
We just want you to see the same light.

Please just listen to the stories we have found,
To the research we have run aground.
We hear you when you say science has its limit,
We just don't believe we aren't within it.

We need you to try
And not to sigh.
Why can't you just concur
That a miracle will occur?

A Question of Faith

Faith of any kind
Is all very fine
When it teaches you to expand your mind,
When it teaches you to be patient,
To be kind,
To share in our humanity
In this world's, too often, cold insanity.

Yet when it is used as a tool
To make you narrow,
And therefore cruel,
To create a you and a them,
The way has been lost
At such a cost.

And no faith can protect
From the most difficult of concepts.
We must be resigned,
For by design
Illness will come to us all.
It is only a matter of time.

For many, illness leads to questions of faith.
Some believe it simply can't be true.
Others, a cure is quite simply their due.
The miracle will happen for you,
If only you pray
Every day,
Because you are you.

Yet faith is not a shield,
Before even which illnesses must yield.
The world's religions teach instead a vision
Of what life can be, if we were all generous, and just
If we could all live in trust.
If we could see the beauty of diversity in our mind,
If we could simply always be kind
The world's religions teach to try to be your best self.
For a life in which you open your shell
Is a life lived well.

Believing you are owed
Is not what faith was ever meant to sow.
Such beliefs do not bring relief,
They often just add grief
At times of illness and pain.
Thinking this way does not create any gains.

For though on Earth we roam,
We will all be called home.
No one knows when
Or how our lives will end.

Coping

This must be the hardest part of your job.
I don't know how you do it;
I just don't know how you get through it.
How do you cope?
How do you not lose hope?

I smile politely;
You ask so nicely.
Yet your questions force me to examine
Things about myself, that I don't even want to imagine.

How do I cope?
How do I still hope?
How do I deal with the high stakes?
How do I deal with the heartbreaks?

I do not know if the answers exist,
But I am filled with dread;
What will I find
If I delve inside my own mind?
Will I be able to escape my own head?
So, I simply persist…

One step in front of the other.
One day at a time, so goes the old rhyme,
But what I do know
To live, is to be present.
Even though it's not always pleasant,
To live each moment as it lasts
Is all we can ever ask.

Goodbye

I wish you could open your eyes one more time.
I wish I could see them shine,
With all your thoughts and emotions.
But the look I most want to see
Is the one you reserve just for me.

I know you are leaving;
It's in all the messages I am receiving.
I wish it was all a bad dream,
I wish nothing is what it seems.

My pain is unmeasurable,
My grief is unbearable;
How can I lose hope?
How will I cope?

I know I just have to look inside my mind
And there, you I will find.
For you have shaped me in ways I can't even begin to define.
Brought out the best in me, made me shine;
Nothing will ever change what I learned from you.
The love we shared will always hold true.

Though I will never be ready,
I promise I will try hard to hold steady.
For none of these facts can be altered
And knowing this I will try not to falter.
You made me who I am, who I want to be;
You let me be me.
If I remember you in all these ways,
With me you will always be.
I will hear what you would say
Until the end of my very own days.

Loss

Life turns over a cruel leaf,
One person lost, another mired in grief.
Mass casualties, nasty viruses, new and old,
Stories, around the world unfold.
Scenes of chaos, fear and exhaustion,
Scenes of courage and collaboration,
Life turns over a misshapen leaf,
No signs of relief,
So many lost, grief, now beyond belief.

How do you cope with such loss?
How do you deal with love's cost?
How do you deal with so much pain?
How is it possible to believe in life again?

Tousled and torn,
Toughened and reborn,
Touched and shaped,
Toughened and scraped,
People in our lives, us, they make.

Why must we say goodbye?
Why must there be so much time to cry?
Why must we go into the storm?
Why does the sun still rise in the morn?

Use memories to learn,
Those lost will always be lights that burn.
Use memories to teach,
Those lost will always be within reach.
Use memories to aspire,
Those lost will always be there to admire.

Ghosts

The ICU is haunted, some people say.
There are ghosts here that just can't find their way
And they seem to be here to stay.

Let me be plain,
Though I don't see how ghosts can be
And it's never happened to me.
There are stories I can't explain.
Don't look at me askance,
For this is not science.

They say in the evening's twilight
And the gloom of the night,
On monitors and machines
Names sometimes appear,
Of people previously seen.
Names of people who have now disappeared.
Names of people who are no longer here.

Some people find it quite disturbing
And others quite unnerving.
If it is true, this is what I will say to you.
I think it's quite nice we sometimes leave behind
An energy that can't be defined.
That tells of who we are and what we shared;
An energy that says we were there.

My poetry

My poetry is deep;
Does it haunt your sleep?

These captured moments in time,
Have been written to help you self-define.

What did your day hold?
How did your life unfold?

Did you have the courage to speak?
Or did you melt away with a squeak?

Did you have the courage to see?
Did you have the courage to be?

What does your heart desire?
What sets your soul on fire?

My poetry is deep;
Does it haunt your sleep?

Last words

Now we are done.

I hope you enjoyed these reflections;
I hope they let us make some connections,
To what is real and true.
To who you are,
To help you find your own North Star.

I hope you better understand
What it's like to hold a life in your hand.
These moments from the ICU
Are my gift to you.

www.ingramcontent.com/pod-product-compliance
Lightning Source LLC
LaVergne TN
LVHW042000060526
838200LV00041B/1799